A SHORT

TO

VENTRILOQUISM

By MAURICE HURLING.
The Voice Illusionist.

British Library Cataloguing-in-Publication Data
A catalogue record for this book is available from the
British Library

Ventriloquism

Ventriloquism, or ventriloquy, is an act of stagecraft in which a person (a ventriloquist) changes his or her voice so that it appears that the voice is coming from elsewhere, usually a puppeteered 'dummy'. The act of ventriloquism is ventriloquizing, and the ability to do so is commonly called in English, the talent to 'throw' one's voice.

Originally, ventriloquism was a religious practice. The name comes from the Latin *to speak from the stomach*, i.e. *venter* (belly) and *loqui* (speak). The Greeks called this gastromancy (Greek: εγγαστριμυθία). The noises produced by the stomach were thought to be the voices of the dead, who took up residence in the stomach of the ventriloquist. The ventriloquist would then interpret the sounds, as they were thought to be able to speak to the dead, as well as foretell the future. One of the earliest recorded group of prophets to utilise this technique was the Pythia, the priestess at the temple of Apollo in Delphi, who acted as the conduit for the Delphic Oracle. In the Middle Ages, such techniques were thought to be similar to witchcraft. As Spiritualism led to stage magic and escapology, so ventriloquism became more of a performance art as, starting around the nineteenth century, it shed its mystical trappings.

The shift from ventriloquism as a manifestation of spiritual forces, toward ventriloquism as entertainment happened in the eighteenth century at the travelling fairs and market towns. The earliest recorded ventriloquists date back to 1753 in England, where Sir John Parnell is depicted in an engraving of William Hogarth, speaking via his hand. In 1757, the Austrian Baron de Mengen implemented a small doll into his performance. By the late eighteenth century, ventriloquist performances were an established form of entertainment in England, although most performers threw their voice to make it appear that it emanated from far away, rather than the modern method of using a puppet. A well known ventriloquist of the period, Joseph Askins, who performed at the Sadler's Wells Theatre in London in the 1790s, advertised his act as 'curious ad libitum dialogues between himself and his invisible familiar, Little Tommy.'

The entertainment came of age during the era of the music hall in the UK and vaudeville in the US. George Sutton began to incorporate a puppet act into his routine at Nottingham in the 1830s, but it is Fred Russel who is regarded as the father of modern ventriloquism. In 1886, he was offered a professional engagement at the Palace Theatre in London and took up his stage career permanently. His act, based on the cheeky-boy dummy 'Coster Joe' that would sit in his lap and 'engage in a dialogue' with him, was highly influential for the entertainment format and was adopted by the next generation of performers.

This arrangement was taken forward by Arthur Prince in the UK, with his dummy Sailor Jim, who became one of the highest paid entertainers on the music hall circuit. In America, the genre was moved on by Frank Byron Jr. and Edgar Bergen, who popularised the idea of the comedic ventriloquist. Bergen, together with his favourite figure, Charlie McCarthy, hosted a radio program that was broadcast from 1937 to 1956.

Ventriloquism's popularity waned for a while, probably because of modern media's electronic ability to convey the illusion of voice, the natural special effect that is the heart of ventriloquism. A number of modern ventriloquists have developed a following though, as the public taste for live comedy grows. In 2001, Angelique Monét performed on Theatre Row, with her one-woman show 'Multiple Me' (written by Edgar Chisholm) where she portrayed several personalities using multiple dummies to display the shifts. In 2007, Zillah & Totte won the first season of *Sweden's Got Talent* and became one of Sweden's most popular family/children entertainers. The art of ventriloquism, it would seem, is still as fresh and as loud today, as it has been in the past.

PREFACE.

Practically everyone will agree, I am sure, that this most interesting Art still retains its fascination and popularity with every section of the public. Although hundreds of years old yet it is ever new.

Probably ninety-nine people out of every hundred believe that VENTRILOQUISM is a GIFT or a special talent bestowed on a lucky few.

Let me explode this fallacy at once. ANYONE, male or female, can certainly learn to become a Ventriloquist providing they have that very necessary virtue PATIENCE and will devote a reasonable amount of time to practice.

One wonders why there are not more Lady Ventriloquists these days. I can imagine some humorist remarking, " Because the Lady couldn't keep her mouth still " or " Because the ' Figure ' would never get a word in edgeways."

But seriously, there is always room in the Entertainment Market for good Ventriloquists of either sex and they can always be sure of a good reception.

In the following pages I am giving you a few Tips on how to become a Ventriloquist. It would take a whole book in itself to go deeply into the subject, but if you will follow my method carefully you will find it a fairly short cut. You should be able to grasp the essential details quite easily and with the necessary practice and polish, put on a show.

A good FIGURE is essential (The " Dummy," not the Performer). Not necessarily expensive, but one with a saucy expression and easily manipulated movements. The " Cheeky Boy " Figure is the most popular for beginners and a really excellent Figure may be obtained from L. DAVENPORT & Co., at a very reasonable price.

I strongly advise the pupil to work with the Figure right from the start and so build up together.

Practice as much as possible in front of a Mirror. You will then see your mistakes and be better able to rectify them. Above all, don't rush things. Start slowly, speed will come later. And thoroughly master each step before proceeding with the next.

Now go ahead with the lessons and remember the more you practice the quicker you will attain your object.

PRELIMINARY EXERCISE.

Stand in front of a mirror, not too close, and let your lips be slightly apart.

Now try to say each letter of the alphabet without any movement of the lips. With very little practice you will soon find you can do this quite easily except for the letters B, M, P. V. and W.

For these:—

B is pronouced " ge "

M   ,,   " EMG "

P   ,,   " KEY "

V   ,,   " VHEE " (breathe it)

W   ,,   " Duggle-you "

You will of course realise you must not blatently say " Key " for P, but make it sound as near P as you can and so on with the others.

Do not slur the letters. Make each one sharp and clear with a short interval between each one.

N.B.—You will find, if your are a smoker, that a cigarette placed between the lips will help to keep them perfectly still.

LESSON I.

Now take your Figure on your knee. Put your forefinger on the lever or in the ring that controls the mouth movement. The other fingers and thumb grasp the pole.

One sharp pull and release at once will work the mouth for each letter.

For the letter W you will have to pull THREE TIMES, once for each sylable.

Now to go through the Alphabet again WITH THE FIGURE, working it as a conversation, but with LETTERS ONLY.

You say A, moving the lips, the Figure says B (lips still) and so on alternately all through.

Now go through again but REVERSE THE ORDER. Let the Figure start with A, you with B, etc.

This exercise should be thoroughly practiced EVERY DAY until you are able to perform this smartly without any mistakes.

LESSON 2.

Now to carry on a step further with the same idea, but introducing a few simple words. The "words" you will notice are after all, just letters when spoken by the Figure.

Practice the following in a conversational manner.

Pupil: Now Tommy, I'm going to have a little chat with you.

Figure: R. U. (Are you).

P. I'm quite in earnest.

F. I. C. U. R. (I see you are).

P. What yould you say if I gave you a shilling?

F. O. G. (Oh! GEE!).

P. That's not an answer.

F. Y. (Why?)

P. Because I say it isn't.

F. O. I. C. (Oh! I see!)

P. If I don't give you a shilling, what shall I give you?

F. An I. O. U.

P. I'm really very generous.

F. I C. U. R. (I See you are).

P. But as we are only rehearsing I'm not really giving you anything at all. NOW what do you think of me?

F. O. U. R. A. J. (Oh, you are a Jay).

LESSON 3.

Up to now you have been speaking in your natural voice both for yourself and for the Figure.

Now we come to one of the most important steps and this is the " other voice," or the voice you will use for the Figure.

It is essential that this should be entirely different from your own, to provide a contrast and create the illusion of two persons speaking.

The " voice " should be produced from the throat without strain.

Obviously you should suit the voice to the Figure. A special chapter could be introduced here on the various kinds of voices and voice production, but I know that the majority of Ventriloquists usually commence with a " Cheeky Boy " Figure and I will proceed on the assumption that you are going to begin in this way.

Experiment with your voice and you will be surprised at the many and varied " tones " or " pitches " you can produce.

For the Cheeky Boy you will need to experiment until you hit on a fairly high pitch, but do not on any account make the voice FALSETTO.

Practice until you hit on a clear HARD tone, either higher or lower than your own.

Make sure you can hit on this just when you want to, without any facial effort or strain.

If you are in doubt about your " voice " let me advise you to have a chat with a boy, ask him a few questions and when he answers TRY TO IMITATE HIS VOICE. You will find this the quickest and easiest way to find a voice for your Figure.

LESSON 4.

It is now necessary to go through the preceding lessons again. But this time make the Figure use the voice you have just found.

You will soon get used to altering the voice quickly and if you have followed out and thoroughly practiced each lesson, you should now be able to carry on a short conversation with your figure.

It is now up to you to enlarge your vocabulary and use more words for the Figure to say. Carry on an impromptu conversation . . . Say anything that comes to your mind and you will find yourself progressing rapidly.

All that is necessary now is to get some life into your work. Keep the Figure on the move by turning the head, eyes, etc. MAKE YOUR FIGURE ACTIVE. Get really smart, snappy jokes and " patter." Work them up until you can say everything CLEARLY and DISTINCTLY. THEN and NOT until then, try your dialogue on a few friends to gain confidence. You should then be ready to look for engagements.

PART II.

NEW & ORIGINAL MATERIAL FOR VENTRILOQUISTS.

1. Miscellaneous Gags and Jokes.

2. An "ALPHABETICAL " item.

3. " I 'aint 'alf a Lad."
   Recitation for FIGURE.

4. " I WISH." Song for Figure.

5. " THE BOXER."
   A NEW & ORIGINAL Ventriloquial Act.

6. HINTS and TIPS.

MISCELLANEOUS.

A — Ventriloquist.   B — FIGURE.

A. I shall be glad when Sunday comes so that we can have a rest.

B. But I don't like Sundays.

A. Why Not?

B. Oh, I DID get in a shocking row last Sunday.

A. Why, whatever happened.

B. Well, you see. I went to Church and got there a bit late.

A. That's very wrong of you.

B. And when I got inside the Church door the Parson was FINISHING HIS SERMON.

A. Good Gracious! A BIT late. Well, go on.

B. Do you know what he said.

A. No.

B. He said, " Stand up, stand up, all of you who would like to go to heaven.

A. Well?

B. Everybody stood up. Then a little later he said, " Now stand up all of you who want to go to the other place."

A. I see.

B. Nobody stood up.

A. Of course not.

B. Well I stood up, and he looked at me and said, " Surely, surely you don't want to go to everlasting Fire? " I said, " No Sir, but I didn't like to see you STANDING UP THERE ALL BY YOURSELF."

A. Why don't you talk Sense?

B. You WOULDN'T UNDERSTAND IT.

A. I suppose you are fond of Football?

B. Rather! When I'm older I'm going to have a FOOTBALL WEDDING.

A. But whatever is a Football Wedding?

B. Well, when I meet the right Girl, one properly dressed, no HALF-BACKS for me, I'll get her in a CORNER and ask her to accompany me to the GOAL of my ambition. Being in LEAGUE with me will make our ASSOCIATION impossible of a DIVISION.

A. Good! Go on.

B. On our wedding day, we shall leave SHEFFIELD UNITED, start from Sheffield WEDNESDAY and go to BLACKPOOL for our HONEYCOMBE.

A. No, no! Honey-MOON.

B. HoneyCOMBE.

A. HoneyMOON.

B. It doesn't matter, they are both " CELLS." There we will become BOLTON WANDERERS through NOTTS FOREST. Then we will BURY all our troubles in our " NEWPORT-manteau "; that is, if it will OLDHAM, if not the lid will have to be PRESTON (pressed on). Then we will go to CAR-DIFF and raise the CUP to our children's future happiness whom she will MOTHERWELL. Then on to BLACKBURN and STOKE the fire in our own little ASTON VILLA and take the AYR, UNITED. Anyone want their Football Coupons filled up?

A. You've got enough WOOD in your head to make a WOODEN KETTLE.

B. You've enough WATER in yours to FILL IT.

A. Where do you work?

B. I don't WORK. I'm in a GOVERNMENT OFFICE.

A. What are you going to be when you are older?

B. I'm going to be a BUTCHER, that's the job to "SUET" me.

A. But you know nothing about it?

B. P'raps not yet, but I do know that my sister's going out with a fellow with MUTTON CHOP whiskers and I can't stand chaps of his KIDNEY.

One day, when I have the HEART I'LL STEAK my life I'll smack his CHOPS and put his LIGHTS out, the saucy SAUSAGE. That will stop him "MEAT-ing" her and perhaps after that he will LIVER alone.

AN ALPHABETICAL ITEM.

B. I feel hungry to-night, Guv'nor.

A. But you ought not to be hungry this time of the day, haven't you had your tea?

B. As a matter of fact I've been all through the alphabet trying to find some food.

A. I don't understand you, explain.

B. Well first of all I went to the A.B.C. restaurant, but all the Waitresses seemed to be D.E.F.

A. I see, Deaf.

B. So I went to the G.H.

A. What's that?

B. The GRAND HOTEL. The Manager looked at me and said, " I.J.K.L."

A. I.J.K.L. What's that?

B. Instantly Journey to the " KAFE LYONS." But I'd only got M.N.

A. M.N.?

B. Yes. Merely Ninepence, so I joined an O.P.Q., that's an "'OT PIE QUEQUE " and when I got in the shop, they'd sold out.

A. Hard luck. What did you do then?

B. I sat down and had an R.S.T.

A. I see, a REST.

B. That's right, and after a little while I said to the girl, thanks for the " rest " and she said U.V.W.

A. What's that mean.

B. U're very welcome.

A. Very well, we'll pass that. What did you do then.

B. I went home, opened a bottle of double X, you ask me Y.

A. Yes?

B. Well there's no more to be Z (said).

" I 'AINT 'ALF A LAD, I AM "

RECITATION FOR FIGURE.

I'm just ten years old, and I 'aint 'alf a Lad,
Sometimes I'm quite good, but I'm more often Bad;
For instance, the other day just before tea,
My Dad came home early, and started on me,
He said " Tommy my Lad," that's ME, you can guess,
" Where is the GLUE? Come along now, confess "
I said " ON YOUR CHAIR DAD, you ARE in a MESS."
Oh I 'aint 'alf a Lad, I am.
Of course after that I was fair in disgrace,
My Dad he was storming all over the place;
He took me upstairs and he gave it me hot,
And said all my fooling he'd jolly soon stop.
He undressed me quick, then to punish me more,
My Dad took my " Nighty," went out of the door,
But I didn't care, I just WENT TO BED RAW.
Oh I 'aint 'alf a Lad, I am.

I think when I'm older I'll have much more sense,
Though of course up to now I'm not DREADFULLY dense;
I SEE things and HEAR things not meant for the young,
Then I get excited and can't hold my tongue.
My MOTHER was ill, and my small sister JOY
Came into this world, just for ME to annoy;
Now DAD's ILL IN BED, I'LL BET IT'S A BOY.
Oh I 'aint 'alf a Lad, I am.

" I WISH "

A concluding song for the Figure.

VERSE.

I wonder if you people ever think of chaps like me,
Though of course there is no reason why you should;
But believe me or believe me not, I wish that I could be
A real live human being, 'stead of WOOD.
I know I'm just a " DUMMY " sitting on my Guv'nor's Knee
That's got no sense or brains or sex appeal,
But I wish that I could LIVE like you and earn some L. S. D.
I feel that I could cry, it seems so REAL.

CHORUS.

I wish that I was made of flesh and blood like you folks here,
I wish that I could EAT and DRINK and SEE and FEEL and
    HEAR,
I wish that I could READ and LEARN and sometimes smoke
    a Fag,
Instead of spending all my time inside my Guv'nor's Bag.
I'm only dragged out now and then when we have got a show
And its ME that does the work, now 'aint that true?
But the Guv'nor gets the CREDIT, and the MONEY, and
    APPLAUSE,
OH! I WISH that I was REAL, Like YOU. .

The above makes an excellent finish for any Act and is
especially suitable for " Vents " that introduce the sobbing or
crying effect.

MUSIC. Full Piano Score may be obtained from . . . .

" THE BOXER "

A NEW & ORIGINAL VENTRILOQUIAL SKETCH.

A. Hello Joe, you look battered. Where is your opponent, in the ring?

B. No, in the HOSPIAL.

A. Did he make a fight of it?

B. He nearly made a MURDER of it.

A. Did you get up at the count of ten?

B. I didn't get up till a quarter past eleven.

A. Another fight like this and your name will be on the headlines.

B. Another fight like that and my name will be on a TOMB-STONE.

A. Tell me? What was your opponent like?

B. You've seen CARNERA?

A. Yes.

B. You've seen King Kong?

A. Yes.

B. He uses them for PUNCHBAGS.

A. Could he punch?

B. Well, I wouldn't call it a punch.

A. What would you call it?

B. An EARTHQUAKE.

A. I suppose when he hit you, your common sense told you what to do?

B. When he hit me I'd NO SENSE left.

A. I suppose you watched his right?

B. That was the trouble.

A. How?

B. While I was watching his RIGHT, he kept hitting me with his LEFT.

A. Were you quick on your feet?

B. So quick, he had a job to catch me.

A. Did your Seconds throw in the Towel?

B. No, they threw ME in instead.

A. Well, I told you what to do before you went in the ring, when he came at you, you should have feinted.

B. I FAINTED THREE TIMES.

A. Did your Seconds bring you to?

B. They didn't even bring me ONE.

A. You could have finished him with a right hook.

B. I couldn't have done it with a BOAT HOOK.

A. How many rounds did you have?

B. THREE, AND A PLATE OF HAM.

A. No, no, I mean Rounds in the fight.

B. I don't know, I was going round all the time.

A. Was the fight for Welter-weight?

B. I think so. He WELTED me alright.

A. Was your opponent a Middle-weight or a Cruiser?

B. I think he was a BATTLESHIP.

A. You shook hands at the start of the fight?

B. Yes, and I've been SHAKING ever since.

A. Did he knock you over?

B. Did he? I was ON MY BACK most of the time.

A. When you lay on your back, what did he say?

B. COME UP AND SEE ME SOMETIME.

A. Well, you wouldn't take any notice of ME. I told you to " lie low " for the first three rounds.

B. I was lying low all through.

A. Why?

B. He wouldn't let me get up.

A. Why didn't you use your head?

B. Because HE kept using it.

A. What for?

B. A PUNCH BALL.

A. I see, and THIS is the result. I get you all keyed up——

B. You've nearly got me LAID UP.

A. I told you to watch me while I gave you the nod.

B. I know, and while I was watching for the nod——

A. Well?

B. He was punching me on the chin.

A. If you had watched me, you would have come out on top.

B. And I came out ON A STRETCHER.

A. Why didn't you use a side-step?

B. It would have been just the same if I'd have used a DOOR-STEP.

A. I'm ashamed of you. You could have eaten the man.

B. I wasn't hungry.

A. You're an idiot; and after all my pains.

B. YOUR pains? What about MINE?

A. Your opponent surprised me.

B. He darn nigh PARALISED ME.

A. I told you to try IN fighting.

B. It would have been all the same if I'd tried BULL FIGHTING.

A. Everything was in your favour at the start. Didn't you hear them cheering you?

B. I thought I heard somebody shout " DUMP HIM."

A. They were cheering you on.

B. I thought they were " BIRDING ME OFF."

A. I really thought you had a PUNCH in ONE hand.

B. You wait until next time. I'll have a HAMMER in BOTH HANDS.

A. At one time it was quite easy for you. His jaw was wide open.

B. And my EYES were BOTH CLOSED.

A. You had no inspiration?

B. I was covered with it.

A. What?

B. PERSPIRATION.

A. You should have stopped his blows.

B. Lummy! I stopped them all.

A. On your Glove?

B. NO. ON MY NOSE.

A. I'm surprised at you, and you talk about BOXING and the LANDS you have fought in; IRELAND; ENGLAND; SCOTLAND. Tell me, which Land have you fought in most?

B. DREAMLAND.

A. And you said you were ready to fight for a Kingdom.

B. I DID fight for a Kingdom nearly.

A. Which Kingdom?

B. KINGDOM COME.

A. And I thought you would go down to posterity.

B. I went down to somebody but THAT WASN'T HIS NAME.

A. Anyhow. I'm going to give you another chance to make good. I'll match you with the Champion; send you down to the seaside in special training quarters; procure you the best sparring partners; and when you beat the champion you will be at the top of the tree.

B. Is that so?

A. And when you are at the top of the tree what will you do?

B. THROW YOU A COCOANUT.

HINTS AND TIPS.

Don't try to talk out of the corner of your mouth. Don't turn YOUR face away from the audience or try to hide it. FACE your audience BOLDLY, keep your Figure ALIVE, and work all your dialogue SMARTLY.

Be on the alert to introduce impromptu gags. A little good-humoured leg pull is always appreciated, but don't be personal.

Never introduce jokes or gags on questionable subjects.

Don't use other Artistes' Gags, or Business. Remember THEY have had to BUY them or ORIGINATE them. YOU DO THE SAME.

FINALLY, if you can't help moving your lips slightly when the Figure is speaking, don't be disheartened. Profit by the experience of a pal of mine whom I will call Mr. X., and keep this up your sleeve for the critic.

Mr. X. was being congratulated on his Ventriloquial powers but was also told that it was noticed his lips moved now and then. Certainly, said Mr. X. I DO THAT ON PURPOSE. You see, I used to go through my Ventriloquial entertainment without moving my lips at all, but it was never appreciated properly so NOW I always move them a little just to PROVE IT IS REALLY I DOING THE WORK.

Now I fully realise that volumes more could be written on the subject of Ventriloquism, but as this is intended as a short cut I sincerely hope you will have had at least a GOOD START.

PRACTICE AND PERSEVERANCE WILL DO THE REST.

VENTRILOQUIAL FIGURES.

1. Messenger Boy 55/-.
2. Sammy Smart Our Bargain Figure 89/6.
3. Willie Winks 73/6.
4. Sammy the Sailor 55/-.
5. Boy Scout 55/-.
6. Coster Joe 55/-.
   Heads from 8/6 to £5.
   Other Figures in stock, £2 2. 0., £3 3. 0., £5 5. 0.

Lightning Source UK Ltd.
Milton Keynes UK
UKOW02f1713130317
296497UK00001B/309/P